SERGE

These Que

BROKEN SLEEP BOOKS

Published 2020,
Broken Sleep Books:
Cornwall / Wales

brokensleepbooks.com

First Edition

Lay out your unrest.

Publisher/Editor: Aaron Kent
Editor: Charlie Baylis

Typeset in UK by Aaron Kent

Broken Sleep Books is committed to
a sustainable future for our planet,
and therefore uses print on
demand publication.

brokensleepbooks@gmail.com

ISBN: 978-1-913642-03-7

Contents

"In his debut chapbook, Serge Ψ Neptune cements his reputation as the Little Merman of British poetry. These are works of joyful, exuberant physicality, of metamorphosis and yearning. The poems take place in a dream-space of infatuation and memory which feels altogether alive and urgent – windows into our full complexity through a vigorously consistent central image. It is always thrilling to witness a writer finding their form and their passion – the leitmotifs you know they're going to tap into forever, refine and make new, inexhaustible as the ocean. Serge Ψ Neptune does so here in poems that are funny, beautiful and enviably phrased and balanced. Even at their most troubled and moving they transfigure the saddest experiences into something dignified and powerful– something we can all use."

- *Luke Kennard*

"Rich and precise - a pamphlet that pulls you into its world, its heady mix of danger and desire, and bravely lays bare the guts, gore and beauty of being alive. These Queer Merboys broke my heart."

- *Ella Frears*

"Serge Ψ Neptune's poems are alert to the blissful possibilities that queer desire unfolds as well as the challenges of living them out. Here 'night sheds / its worm skin, its polluted armour' but all is never quite as it seems. His mermen discover glittering surfaces but also dark, terrifying water. The tight focus of Serge's attention, however, means his metaphors work in unison, their cumulative effect taking the reader ever deeper into a parallel universe imagined in vivid and thrilling detail."

- *John McCullough*

These Queer Merboys

Serge Ψ Neptune

A Queerness of Mermen

When a squabble of seagulls draws near
the sky is a ceiling of white paper cuts.
One seagull flies a little further
on the shore to feast in solitude,
sits on an anchor & dips
his beak into some fish.
The moon's orchid
dribbles on the cliffs,
a Cornish landscape.

A choir lifts in the distance,
a song of brethren – the mermen's voices
inundate the air.
Gathered on a Friday night
they celebrate themselves – tails sheathed
in Murano glass scales, fins serpentine
as fleurs de lis.
A smack of jellyfish rises up
to shake the seacrest.

When music dwindles down & giggles
grow more sonorous,
the lyres set aside, the flutes abandoned,
& touch becomes a flurry
of honeyed fingers,
a gentle grasp turns firmer.
Lips widen into smiles, kisses change
to playful bites, arms clasp torsos,
fingers hair & mouths let out a sigh.

A sailor peering from a hidden spot
comes out & joins them, disappears
below & is never seen again.
A merman finds a stranded sock,
black scab on the shoreskin, feels

for the first time the touch
of fabric, juggles it
from hand to hand, then wears it
as a glove to give it words.

A Mermen Choir: Far out in the Ocean, Where Water

is murky as
the murkiest
of fogs thick
with shades
of blue in the
deepest of
depths where
a hundred
staircases
would fail
to connect
the ground
with the surface
above slick
with petrol
deep where
currents shake
the flora alive
like flame
deep where
the tittering
of waves blends
yesterday's
sand with
new detritus
& plastic
there sons
& daughters
of this filthy
water forgotten
specimens
there
with lassitude
& grace
we swim

Pietà with Merman and Drowned Body

... tail cleft in grieving reverence... i am the
parlance of the drowned, their gasps and
mutterings... crippled venus full of grace... i am
tilda swinton posing naked on a marble pillar at
the tate... an urchin carried by the waves...
polyphony of plankton, a lovesong to the lost
shore... the stringencies of vapours... vapours
oozing from volcanoes like a thick mantle...
these chemicals affect the coral fauna... body
pushed down by zesty currents... sinking with
poise... hand that fiddles with the depth,
dismissive gesture... a seabed paved with
clams... i am impertinent and my surface
crackles... seanight's turmoil... the to's and fro's
of fish shoals... pretentious carcass... feigning
gently... in drooping pose... bubbles dancing up
the stiffened throat... like guilty guests sneaking
from a party... bottles, rubber tyres, oil rigs,
sunken cathedrals... by the edge of a crevice
anemones dangerously bloom... weary, pale and
restless... fingers of the dead... a worn out
valise floats randomly, shaken in mid-water...
the moment made of light when you
precipitate... tumble down... urgent... unto
these shaky hands... the wrists bending, finally,
to hold you... tail wrapping around to keep you
warm...

These Queer Merboys

can't get any rest
in this depth   lamentous with   waves' slosh
their skins so   mother-of-pearl
& others'   sombre ebony
some have never felt sunlight,
some absorbed   darkness from the abyss
laid on tiny grains   & pebbles,
a Flemish painting of vivid blues
                    cerulean   silks of sand
& waves   sapphire   lapis   emerald
wild fish & cephalopods

*

the older ones warned them that scales would grow restless
            tails twist
in tremor   cheeks farouche with first blushes
            that melt each member down   to the cartilaginous core

bodies have uses   other than swimming
if caught in fishnets   things would happen

            they've all heard the stories
of sailors from land with expert hands that know
            what to do
                        where to touch

*

men took us in their arms   cuddled us at first
            lips fastened to lips
we begged
            for hands to hold our throats feet press on our faces
we will be docile our tongues laid out like summer

throats agape & ruby
limbs scattered   a kitsch souvenir   or under glass
for study & observation

the sea sprinkled with jetsam
caudal fins operculum gills epidermis

look at what's left of us

in the cold   distance

loathsome

& rancorous lovers

An Infancy of Mermen

Remember when tempest gouged the skies like a praying mantis,
how it stretched its hand of wind to grasp the ships and push them down
so deep as to erase their history? Nan told us the men that came from there,

stone-cold and breathless, were the only ones worth loving.
Nan who punished us with ease, and when we threw a tantrum locked us
in a cave of jellyfish, the scars left were many and they burned for days.

Nan who fancied for herself a skin of pearl, the white from the egg of a land bird
to rest on her face before sleep. Nan who taught us to dance,
to follow the tango of octopods, their kiss of arms opening into vast arcades.

Remember the headache, twisting the lobes of our brains like a Rubik's cube?
A whole choir of pain, all female cast, the bone and muscle clattered
their burning out with tongues buttered in B flat. Only Nan knew how to quieten it.

She blessed water in snow-bud china, chanted the names of all her lost lovers,
then kissed our brows to take the pain inside her, chisel it back to a gorgeous silence.
When we came of age, she imposed on us the burden of beauty – *Don't slouch!*

Posture is everything! Wear a corset. If your figure requires it
break a couple of ribs or more. At last she ordered eight big oysters,
the kind of expensive delicacy humans prey on, to show our high rank

they clutched hard to our flesh till the scales bled, and they hurt us so.

A Mermen Choir: How we First came to Land

human experience is one of
disease you wouldn't remember us
first crawling out of water
panting for air in fierce
spasms the pain we knew
water no longer being our
mother giving up our gills
and growing porous bags to
breath swapping our one extremity
for two less silver and
more skin found refuge in
cracked lumps in the darkness
of the ground then behold –
our looks of wonder when
facing the first leap of flame

And if we Wanted to Perambulate like Humans do

The potion they served us, like surgeons,
cut through our blood with irons,
parted our spine like a vision of saints.

Beloved, if only you knew, how my fishtail
splits for you with this desire I can no longer name,
how its sword slashes me into two weaker halves.

Scales would fall, fins harden into bones.
Each step felt like a pig's heart skewered with nails,
like putting one's sole on a carpet of blades.

In the end we discovered our princes as whimsical,
how freedom made them rainbow-feathered birds
that leap from rose to lily without a care.

There's a Tank at London Aquarium, Near the Sharks

filled with mermen, and people observe with their mouths wide open how the mermen flex their tails and plunge, such movements, such colours, such gleaming scales like sequins on a ball gown refracting light, Hollywood smiles and giddy faces, the agility they jump and glide with and how they carry themselves, with seaweed and seashells around their necks and arms, the same glamour stage stars wear neck-laces and feather boas with, and you can afford to stay too close to the glass as the mermen are not threatening and the audience watching is really entertained

look, now a merman offers another a flower as if they're courting and they look into each other's eyes and smile and take each other's hand; *it's almost like real life* says Amanda; Hannah and Will's enchanted faces shine with stupor; they have just bought their first house in Buckinghamshire and come here to celebrate, while Sharon, who has been crying all night, and just met with Kate and Kate asked *do you wanna talk about it?* but now they both laugh and look upwards, the mermen splashing so hard that water sprinkles on kids' faces; a family from Norwich laugh so hard and Billie just arrived as he got distracted by the skate tank, even Karen, who's found a 90's tamagotchi in her attic and has been playing with it all day, has stopped playing and now joins the crowd with her snorting laughter, and in the after-noon some Americans lost their way searching for the big squid but they stayed and enjoyed the display

and in the end, the lights soften and the mermen prepare for sleep and two mermen lie in each other's arms, their tails gently entwined in caduceus fashion, and the audience goes *aaaaw* and thinks it's cute, then everybody proceeds towards the exit.

A Child Comes Out as a Merman

When right after sunset darkness landed on our living room
like a butterfly on an open flower,
mother didn't bother to switch on the lights
and kept watching the telly, laid on our sofa.
The telly blasting *SINNERS! SINNERS!*
While standing by the threshold to the kitchen,
I announced – my voice all jelly – *I am a merman now!*
and mother looked at me for a second, nodded
and tucked her lips again into a blanket of silence.
The morning after I found a leaflet next to my pillow,
content I could not decipher, with pictures as bright
as sun-filled bubbles of morality. Mother said
if I wanted to learn how to swim, they'd pay for lessons.
Dad in the car pestered me with lectures about being
only thirteen and knowing nothing, being full of nothing.
You shall not lie with a creature of the sea, for they have no soul
and only by marrying a creature of land, may they acquire one
I started taking baths before sleep and went to bed
so wet I'd soak the sheets.
Then started sleeping in the bathtub all night.
I joined my legs tight with an elastic band,
enjoyed every cramp, every cold shiver.
The next day screams and thumps out of the bathroom door
woke me up, as I delayed everyone's morning routine.
Over breakfast, mother insisted, once more, I was clueless.
I said I'd found a new god, one more tender,
one that allowed for mellowness.
Mother shook her head, dad shouted to go to my room,
called me an abomination.
I refused to eat their food, I asked mother to cook seaweed.
They decided to leave me alone, a shadow sewing
button-eyes on ghost dolls. No one took a bath in the evening.
They noticed me less and less.
Once, they watched a stand-up show on the telly, had their chests
shake with so much laughter, they couldn't hear a thing.
Once the water in my bathtub was all cherry, I tried to stop
the flowers of my wrists from blossoming.

A Mermen Choir: Let a Tap Left Dripping Overnight

be our lovesong
no death is sweeter
than a death in our arms
man of land man
of many labours
remember the younger
days discovering
the frailties of
your body
the embarrassment
of communal showers
those pressured
tiny licks like
hands touching
every inch of skin
even now you dream
the same dream
or maybe you're literally
sinking
our lips
grazing yours
our tongues pushed
down your throat
quite forcefully
like water flooding
the collapsing
temple of yourself

The Merman has had a Plethora of Boyfriends

The first boyfriend wonders how sex should work.
There must be among these scales an opening to pleasure.

The second boyfriend gives the merman syphilis, in Hólmavík,
in the public toilets of the museum of Icelandic Witchcraft & Sorcery.

With the third boyfriend the merman starts to cling
to whatever mirrors reflect the part of himself he wants to be true.

Show me how to use that knife, the merman says to the fourth boyfriend
and watches as he applies the blade to the wrists like a soothing balm.

You'll get your money back, the merman reassures the fifth boyfriend, I just need time.

You mermen can be real tossers sometimes, shouts the sixth boyfriend.

To the seventh boyfriend, the merman explains why life under sea has its issues that so much solitude leads to an apnea of feelings that cools the heart to an icicle.

Being with the eighth boyfriend is like launching a new form of sex that's already obsolete, a dead-end to a newborn relationship.

Don't hold out on me, says the merman to the ninth boyfriend, tell me what you really like. Right now, in some very tiny flats in Japan, young couples are resorting to octopuses to revive their passion.

Think of this as couples therapy, he said

Love is a recipe you should approach with care.
One must respect its religion,
every ritual gesture adding up to the final flavour.

He dismantled the fish carcass,
removed spine and skin,
how the cobweb of its blood
branched out across the pulp in tiny streams.

He added the fish flakes to the saucepan
filled with milk and vegetables,
kept all the utensils by his side.

How each piece slowly blended to the next
the way vines entwine to one another
until no wall is left.

By then, the kitchen was a limp joke of moisture.
He glided in the steam like a starfish
and I sat – his prey, waiting for him
to pull his inners out and suckle on my tissue,
every stomach gland fizzing with joy.

The Merman Tells us About a Dinner Date gone, oh, so Wrong

I stabbed my hand with a kitchen knife and screamed as you ran to grab a napkin. As you opened the drawer I stabbed my hand a second time to find out how much of myself I could hold together as a single unity of pain. You came back with a blood-red napkin from new year's eve, sifting the air with it like a matador, and tried to choke the pit of my wound that wouldn't stop overflowing, holding down my arm. My hand chakra might be damaged forever. You sat me in your car and informed me about how much it would cost to clean these seats. I lifted my arm and could see the plum of the moon, sweating light off albino pores through the hole in my hand and directly into my eye. The nurses confabulated at the front desk, while a guy, looking like a Shaman, played his drums in the corner near the vending machine. Even with no documents, I was taken in. I shouted at the sight of the knife, so they brought a spoon instead and all I ate was jelly. They left me with a bandage, a glass of water on my bedside and a couple of white pills, tiny full moons of good-riddance.

The Floating Game

Mr. Barnum, the circus master, repeats once more he's worried!
I should take better care of my tail; – the scales have lost their shine;

parasites spread on fins – laceration and loss of skin may follow.
Uncertain on whether vet or physician can provide the right fix,

they feed me pills to fill the chamber of my brain with smoke.
Here in the tank where I only swim in circles, tense with boredom,

wondering if by now the sky is a post-apocalyptic amber stuffed with bugs
or grim like the top shelf up there you haven't dusted in ages.

A new day entails a new display of eccentricities, the wild & exotic
caged tight & well so spectators feel safe. By now I master

the concrete art of raising a smile upon demand – look! The crowd
of monkeys cheerfully pointing at me, as if I am the strange one.

When not cooperating, they'll leave low voltage electrodes in water,
a fuzzy assemblage of nauseous fits. When cleaning or bringing food,

they'll arrive with wax stuck in their ears, scared I may hum a few notes.
Every day I practice total immobility, stillness worthy of a Zen master,

and float like that goldfish your kid has forgotten to feed for an entire week.
Now, picture the scene: Mr. Barnum coming closer to check on his motionless

specimen. Picture him as he slowly opens the tank. Now – a sudden leap!
Teeth arrayed about his throat, refusing to let go

Last time my Lover came Inside me

after months we hadn't seen each other
and thirst gripped his throat,
he seemed anxious, impatient to reassure me

- that *they* were happy
- that *she* made him happy
- that her milk-flood skin was enough,
  even when it failed
  to arouse him.

When he pounded full-force inside me
he shouted her name,
yet he moaned at the brusque
friction of my scales,
my viscous fishtail
that coiled around his waist.

I would wear him all over me
like a lilac-red blanket
as if love had flayed him,
lively and scorched.

The scent of my bearded face
dragged him to the maelstrom of my tongue,
my echo of spite followed him
free till morning.

And the wife had warned him
about the mermen that crept below the tide
or jumped off big-city puddles,
that waited behind lurid cliffs to pull men
down to the estuary's depths
or cause a shipwreck with their venom-song,

and if ever caught he'll say

- that he's been coaxed
  and vexed
- that he meant for none of this
  to happen
- that my kelp-blue touch did nothing,
  proved nothing
  to him,
  to others.

A Mermen Choir: 'We Know Plenty of How Men...'

spread their masculinity
we know they've
got a tendency
to waste away
in their liberty
rain their eyes
down to droplets
with no mind
for those who
love them
kiss them
while they
sleep or dream
they drain
the sweat
of salty lovers
on their lips
their sighs
are gravestones
gravestones on our
gliding fins
they scratch
move out in packs
men rape us
- give us peace -
let our bodies
cease existing
our burdens
give way
scales are suddenly
more viscous
kill our lovers before
our hearts are broken
half of our flesh
if ever eaten
will taste bitter
with deceit

Melusine Boys

Come high tide the sea filled us with screams
& gave us nightmares,
scuppered our lust so we grew up tainted, always
pining for the wrong men.
The bankmen, the office workers,
doctors & lawyers
have kissed their kids goodnight & come to find us.
They know the spot.

Lads that would climb mountains for us.
Some have waited
patiently, saving carefully, hiding the money
from their wives.
Lost in the boroughs and narrow alleys, men
came & went
until their names grew pale as clouds,
then slowly faded.

They fell for our finned hands & feet,
our scaly legs,
called us the nymphette-boys of Greek st.
Upon finding
they'd been sea-lured, shame hit like a ram's
bright head
& they built high pyres of the driest wood,
for our pain to last long & red.

The men that once had bedded us now chained us
to the stakes,
tucked us in engulfing flame. Before demise
we sang
to them a song so sweet & blithe they'd dream of it,
& at the apex
of our highest note they followed us into the fire
& burned with us.

And When she Caught us in our Heartache, the Sea Witch Said

if
you kill
the man you love
& pour the blood
from his heart
onto your legs,
they will
join
into
a tail
a   gain.

How Sailors at Sea Mistook Manatees for Mermen

i

sea wrapped in itself like a dead bug
voyaged on sunk within its liquorish water
that once drunk burns the mouth elongated
bone-structure of the sea its drench bark
zappy whirlpool skin cosy exoskeleton even
the greatest of men here flounder

ii

how long to be lost at sea months years
hormones spiral mind hallucinates how the
absence of touch dictates what one sees in a
distance of waves ~~ one defines lust as a
sea cucumber wriggling inside the ear & into
the brain ~~

what factors contribute to the brain splitting
into chunks of desire a ship that wobbles this
loneliness of salt that tastes like pork well
past its due date & the other sea mammals
~~ gaily swimming by

iii

brine-lustrous species head & trunk of man
ending in a tail of fish or cetacean these
beguilers test the thirst of men lips wet with
prophecy which have had centuries to
practice teasing scaly Cassandras nobody
ever listens to for fear of drowning & what
is it to love a man if not to drag him
underwater to steal his last breath

every sea-faring culture reporting the cheek
of it

iv

the sun like a spell of sweat which blurs the
sight the motions of shoulders pulling ropes
vigour of firm hands make a man forget
himself how a secret peek can cause the
strongest lungs to bruise

when tempest arrives it's a quarrel of
spinster clouds fighting over the most
handsome sailors waves become hands that
clutch & crush & when wood turns to
splinters men look for each other ~~ not
even the virile want to die alone or unloved
when you drown you can feel the brain of
the sea at work hear its synapses cling to one
another like a fishnet of laughter & song ~~

v
everything so blue wish I could eat the blue
whole like a pretty blue hamburger have you
ever chewed on your own guilt how a song
pulls and twists the mind of a man so that he
wants to die to forget his home & family our
voices' frills baroque jukebox our lips know
~~ the wants of flesh

but what survives of us once men forget
little brothers we flick our fins in spite
dissolve sperm-white glowing spume on
choppy waves first wink of dawn

The Beginning of Dawn

In those thin hours when night sheds
its worm skin, its polluted armour,

when lamplights switch off and go home
to some hypothetical realm of lamplights,

when amber wrestles with rose
and dampens the sky with colour, in a city

that once whispered *I love you* the same way he did
on a ferry boat sulking on the Thames.

Acknowledgements

Thank you to the editors of the following publications in which some versions of these poems have appeared: *Harana Poetry, whynow, Lighthouse, Banshee,* and *Brittle Star.*

I would like to thank all the poets and mentors that supported me and believed in my work: Melissa, Luke, Ella, John, Sarah, Katy, Wayne, Lisa, Astra, Alice, Nicki, Tristram, Kostya, Eddus, Joe, Jacqueline, and especially Richard Scott, who remains my greatest inspiration.

Thanks to my family and friends, especially Jonna, Daniel, Ashley, Amy, Laura, Aina, Sasha, Edweena, Rob, Ciaran, and Rasa.

An especially big thank you to Aaron and Charlie.

LAY OUT YOUR UNREST

Lightning Source UK Ltd.
Milton Keynes UK
UKHW020918050520
362800UK00005B/159

Planets

Illustrated by Rob Jakeway

OXFORD
UNIVERSITY PRESS

This book belongs to

OXFORD
UNIVERSITY PRESS

Great Clarendon Street, Oxford OX2 6DP

Oxford University Press is a department of the University of Oxford.
It furthers the University's objective of excellence in research, scholarship,
and education by publishing worldwide in

Oxford New York

Auckland Bangkok Buenos Aires Cape Town Chennai
Dar es Salaam Delhi Hong Kong Istanbul Karachi Kolkata
Kuala Lumpur Madrid Melbourne Mexico City Mumbai Nairobi
São Paulo Shanghai Singapore Taipei Tokyo Toronto

Oxford is a registered trade mark of Oxford University Press
in the UK and in certain other countries

British Library Cataloguing in Publication Data available

Paperback ISBN 0–19–910749–1

3 5 7 9 10 8 6 4 2

Printed in Spain by Edelvives

Contents

▶ Voyage into space

ZOOOOOOM!

Hold tight as our spaceship flies through space! Look down there – where are we?

That is the planet Mercury, the first stop on our journey. Mercury is the planet nearest to the sun. Let's orbit round a few times.

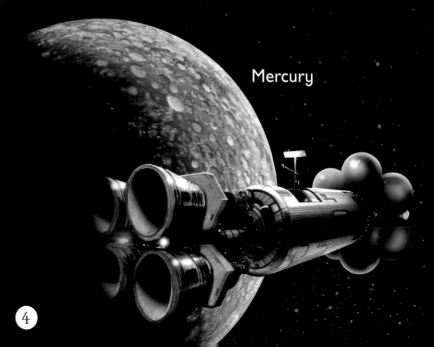

Mercury

From Mercury the sun looks enormous in the jet-black sky. This is a grey world, with dusty plains, high cliffs and huge craters.

It's not safe to land the spaceship. There's no air out there, and it's **HOT!** Hotter than the hottest oven. A pizza would burn to a crisp in seconds!

But at night it will get really **COLD.** Much colder than ice.

Altogether there are nine planets circling our sun. They are:

Venus **M**ars

Mercury **E**arth **J**upiter

the sun

One way to remember the planets in the right order is to make up a sentence using the first letters. Here's an example:

Many **V**ery **E**xcited **M**ammoths **J**umping and **S**kipping **U**phill in **N**ew **P**yjamas.

Perhaps you could make up your own sentence?

Saturn

Neptune

Pluto

Uranus

A real journey to visit all the planets would take many years. By the time we returned you would be grown up!

Luckily, we can pretend. Which planet is next to Mercury?

Did you know...
A planet is a big ball of rock or gas that orbits the sun. As the planet travels it spins like a top. The time it takes for a planet to spin round once is the length of one day for that planet.

▶ Beautiful Venus

Look! There's Venus!

It looks beautiful with its cream-coloured clouds, but it is a very scary place. Down under those pretty clouds it is hot enough to melt metal, and it is impossible to breathe.

Drops of acid, strong enough to eat through rock, fall from the clouds. Thunder roars and lightning flashes in the orange sky, and there are thousands of volcanoes!

surface of Venus

The force of those pretty clouds pressing down on Venus is enough to crush a car – easily! Try putting your hand inside a rubber glove, then hold it under water. Can you feel the force of the water pressing on the glove? That is how the clouds press down on Venus – but MUCH harder!

Did you know...
On Venus the sun rises in the west and sets in the east. This is the opposite to what happens on Earth. It happens because Venus spins in the opposite direction to Earth.

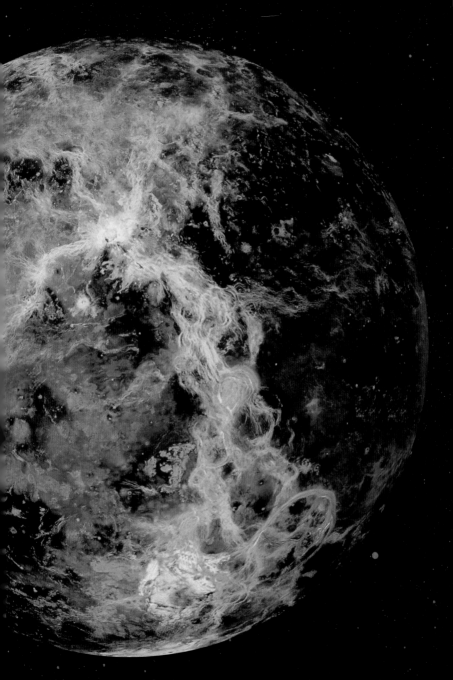

Venus beneath the clouds

▶ Home, sweet home

Now we are passing a beautiful planet. Do you recognize it? That is our Earth!

Earth is the only one of the nine planets where there are plants and animals. That is because it is just the right distance from the sun. It is not too hot and not too cold. There is plenty of water, and air that we can breathe.

But it's not time to go home yet. There are more planets to see!

The red planet

The next planet is Mars. Why do you think it is called the red planet?

The surface of Mars is like a cold, dry desert. There are rocks and boulders everywhere, and the ground is covered with red dust. There are huge mountains and deep valleys, and the sky looks pink.

surface of Mars

There are marks
on the ground
that look like
river beds.
Perhaps millions
of years ago there
were rivers on Mars,
but now it is completely dry.
And freezing. **Brrrrrr!**

Luckily we can keep warm inside
our spaceship as we head for
another planet.

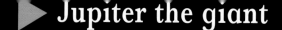

Jupiter the giant

Wow! Look at that! It's **ENORMOUS!**

Jupiter is the biggest planet. It is so big that more than 1000 planets the size of Earth could fit inside it. Jupiter is made of gas, so there is no solid surface to land on, even if we wanted to.

surface of Jupiter

Look at the
orange, brown
and red clouds,
swirling and
changing all the time. Do you see
the red spot on Jupiter? The spot is
a very violent storm, like a tornado.

Gales and hurricanes blow here all
the time, and it is very cold. Much
colder than inside a deep freeze.
Let's go!

Did you know...
Jupiter spins faster
than any other
planet. A day on
Jupiter is only ten
hours long!

Rings round Saturn

The next planet is Saturn. It's easy to recognize because of those broad, bright rings.

Saturn's rings

Scientists think the rings are made of lumps of ice and rock. Some of the lumps are as big as houses, others as small as dust, circling Saturn like a blizzard.

19

Saturn looks very peaceful with its
creamy yellow clouds, but sometimes
there are sudden storms with winds
blowing over 1000 miles per hour.

Did you know...
Saturn has eighteen
moons. Our planet
Earth only has one.

Enough to
blow your
house across
the town!

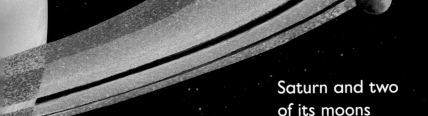

Saturn and two
of its moons

▶ The faraway planets

As we speed further into space the
sun looks smaller and smaller.
Because the sun is so far away it is
very cold out here.

the sun

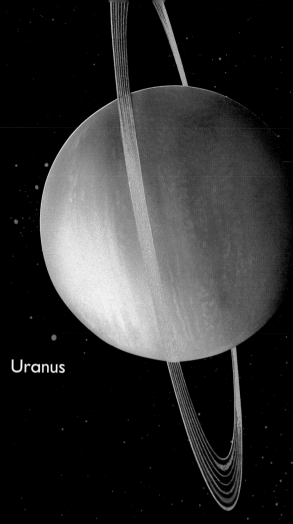

Uranus

This lovely pale greenish-blue planet is Uranus. Have you noticed that it spins on its side? It means that while one half of Uranus has 42 years of daylight, the other half has 42 years of darkness. Can you imagine that?

The next planet is spinning the right way up! Neptune is as blue as the ocean, with clouds and swirling tornadoes. One Neptune year is as long as 165 Earth years. Longer than anyone on Earth has ever lived!

Neptune

The last planet is Pluto, the smallest planet. There it is, far away in the distance. It's a tiny world of rock and ice – or so scientists believe. Pluto is so far away that no spacecraft has ever seen it close up. Perhaps one day, when you have grown up, scientists will know more.

Pluto and its moon

▶ The return journey

Before we go, look out at all those
stars twinkling in the darkness.
Did you know that our sun is a star,
just like billions of others?

Maybe some of those other stars could have planets circling around them. And one of those planets could be just the right distance from its star to have water and air. And maybe, just maybe, there could be life on that planet, just like on Earth. Think of that, next time you gaze up at the sky on a starry night!

As we head back home to Earth, we zoom past the planets once again. Can you recognize this one?

Now our journey's nearly over.
Hold tight! We're going to land – in
the ocean...

SPLOSH!

▶ Planet facts

Below is a table of things you might like to know about the planets.

	Mercury	Venus	Earth	Mars
	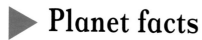			
Length of day*	59 days	243 days	24 hours	24 hours 37 minutes
Length of year*	88 days	225 days	365 days	687 days
Average Temperature	427°C day -170°C night	480°C	22°C	-23°C
Air we can breathe	no	no	yes	no
Water	no	no	yes	no
Number of moons	0	0	1	2
Distance from sun (million km)	58	108	150	228
Relative size	orange pip	small grape	grape	pea

*Earth days/hours/minutes)

Remember, a day is the length of time
it takes a planet to spin round once.
A year is the length of time it takes for
a planet to travel round the sun.

Jupiter	Saturn	Uranus	Neptune	Pluto
10 hours	10 hours 14 minutes	17 hours 54 minutes	19 hours 12 minutes	6 days
12 years	29 years	84 years	165 years	248 years
-150°C	-180°C	-210°C	-220°C	-230°C
no	no	no	no	no
no	no	no	no	no
16	18	15	8	1
778	1,427	2,869	4,496	5,900
small melon	grapefruit	lime	tomato	peppercorn

▶ Glossary

This glossary will help you to understand what some important words mean. You can find them in this book by using the page numbers given below.

 acid An acid is a sort of chemical. Strong acids are so dangerous they can burn your skin or eat into rock. **9**

crater A crater is a big hole which has been made by something heavy hitting the ground. **5**

gas Gas is like air. It can move about to fill up any space. Many gases are invisible, but some are coloured, and some are smelly. **7, 16**

moon   A moon is a ball of rock that circles round a planet. Earth has one moon, which you can see in the sky at night.   **20, 28**

orbit   An orbit is the invisible path travelled by a planet as it circles the sun. We can say that a planet orbits the sun.   **4, 7**

star   A star is a big ball of hot, glowing gas in space. Stars give out light and heat. You can see them twinkling in the sky at night.   **25, 26**

sun   The sun is a star. It's nearer to Earth than any other star. It gives us warmth and light.

4, 5, 6, 7, 11, 13, 21, 25, 28, 29

tornado   A tornado is a very strong wind that whirls round in circles.   **17, 23**

Reading Together

Oxford Reds have been written by leading children's authors who have a passion for particular non-fiction subjects. So as well as up-to-date information, fascinating facts and stunning pictures, these books provide powerful writing which draws the reader into the text.

Oxford Reds are written in simple language, checked by educational advisors. There is plenty of repetition of words and phrases, and all technical words are explained. They are an ideal vehicle for helping your child develop a love of reading – by building fluency, confidence and enjoyment.

You can help your child by reading the first few pages out loud, then encourage him or her to continue alone. You could share the reading by taking turns to read a page or two. Or you could read the whole book aloud, so your child knows it well before tackling it alone.

Oxford Reds will help your child develop a love of reading and a lasting curiosity about the world we live in.

Sue Palmer
Writer and Literacy Consultant